Lorren Arezio

Be With Me

illustrated by Julia Schigal

First Printed in 2024

Be With Me
© Lorren Arezio, 2024

This book is copyright. Apart from any fair dealing for
the purposes of private study, research, criticism or review, as
permitted under the Australian Copyright Act, no part
of this book may be reproduced, stored in a retrieval system, or
transmitted in any form or by any means, electronic, mechanical,
photocopying, recording or otherwise, without the prior written
permission of the author.

Lorren Arezio is recognised at the creator of this content and has
asserted her right to be identified as the author of this work.

National Library of Australia Cataloguing - in - Publication data:

Arezio, Lorren Be With Me

ISBN: 978-1-7640864-2-4

Printed and distributed by
LightningSource Pty Ltd (IngramSpark)

This book is dedicated to all the children I have had the pleasure of meeting, who struggle with their big emotions, and who need someone to understand and just be with them, without expectation, for as long as it takes.

Some days Echidna wakes up feeling happy.

He likes those days. Anything feels possible.

Maybe today he will fly to the moon.

Or build the biggest tower.

And his little brother won't even mess things up.

That would be AMAZING!

But some days Echidna does not feel happy.

Not one teeny tiny bit!

Some days he just feels cross and grumpy.
Everything feels bad.

These days do not feel like amazing days.
They feel like the worst day ever!

Sometimes there is a reason for feeling this way.

But sometimes there is no reason at all.

Echidna just wakes up feeling this way.

He tries really, really hard not to be grumpy.

But it is too hard to switch it off all by himself.

And that makes him even more mad.

Sometimes he tries to give his Cross and Grumpy to someone else, or to everyone else!

He thinks that if he can make others feel as cross and grumpy as he does, then that will make him feel better.

But it doesn't.

The Cross and Grumpy just stays!

Like something that gets stuck on your foot.

Or a bad smell you can't get rid of.

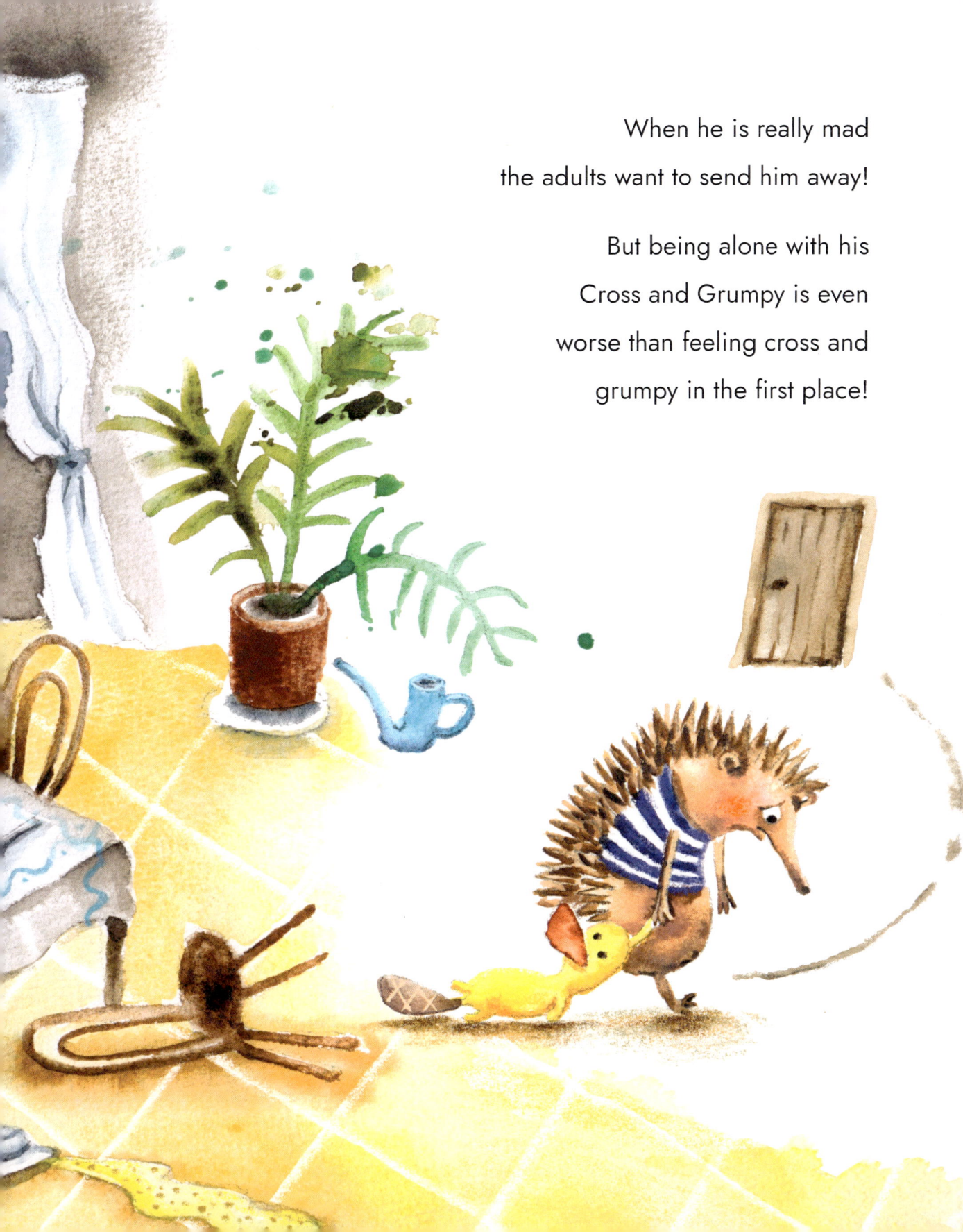

When he is really mad the adults want to send him away!

But being alone with his Cross and Grumpy is even worse than feeling cross and grumpy in the first place!

But deep inside, Echidna worries maybe there might be something wrong with him.

That he will never be OK.

When he feels like this,
he really wants someone to be with him.
To tell him with their eyes that they care. To
pull funny faces with him.

But not if Echidna does not want them to.

Echidna wants someone to just be with him.

For as long as it takes.

Even if they are then late for something.

Or everything!

To go slow and not be in a rush.

And even though they may just sit in silence.
And even though Echidna may still be cross
and grumpy for a while.
Or say "GO AWAY!"

Echidna does not really want them to go. He really wants them to stay.

Because having them sit with him,
and share his Cross and Grumpy,
makes things feel so much better.

And when the adults sit with Echidna,
and just be with him for as long as he needs,
slowly Echidna learns that feelings
are not so scary after all.

Echidna still forgets sometimes.

He tries to fix his Cross and Grumpy all by himself.

He is still growing, and needs more help and practice.

But slowly, Echidna is learning

that when he can be with someone, someone

who is not scared of his mad,

who can help him to understand his feelings,

then he really does feel so much better.

And that just maybe,

he really is OK.

And there is nothing

wrong with him after all.

Well done Echidna!

We are so proud of you.

NOTE FOR THE ADULTS CARING FOR LITTLE ECHIDNAS

Children struggle with feelings and emotions for many reasons. It may be due to anxiety or feeling an expectation from others that they need to be a certain way.

Sometimes it is due to feeling rushed and the pressure that creates. Sometimes it is caused by tiredness, hunger or having sensory overload. Sometimes it is because friendships are hard, or managing siblings is hard, or things have not gone as planned, or they have made a mistake and are feeling embarrassed. Sometimes it can be due to struggles arising from a transition from one activity to another. And sometimes it may be caused by a deeper underlying trauma and deep inner shame that has been triggered within them.

Regardless of the reason, children often have trouble understanding and putting into words what it is they are feeling. And let's face it, feelings are strong and complex at times and our little people need us and our brains to help them make sense of it all.

As adults, we sometimes live in a world of hurry and busy that does not always align with the experiences of our little people. We are moving too fast - onto the next thing - when they are having trouble getting started.

It is easy for us to want to push them along, to reason with them, to tell them what is important, to try to switch off what they are feeling, because we don't have time or energy for a big outburst. However, the truth is that all feelings are valid and emotions need to be worked through.

We may want to teach our children alternate and more helpful ways of expressing what they are feeling. To do this well, we need to sit with them in what they are feeling and help them hold and process the emotions.

When we as adults can slow down and remain present and regulated, our children can feel safe enough to talk about what they are feeling and begin to understand their emotions. Only when they feel supported in this way, can they take on new learnings and know how to handle their emotions next time.

Lorren Arezio is a registered Psychologist, working in Brisbane, Australia.

She has a Master's Degree in Clinical Psychology and has worked with children and families for many years in both public health and private settings.

Lorren has extensive experience in the area of child protection, providing support and therapy to children, families, foster carers, and other professional staff in order to help children to heal and grow.

She is also experienced in supporting families (adults and children) through transitions, life disruption, managing stress, anxiety and parenting challenges. Lorren works through an attachment and trauma lens, and has specialised in Dyadic Developmental Psychotherapy, Practice and Parenting (DDP).

In addition to the above, Lorren maintains a strong interest in adoption, as a mother of three now adult children, the youngest of whom was adopted.

This combined experience has enabled Lorren to understand first hand many of the struggles and difficulties experienced by children and families as they navigate through various life challenges. Lorren brings this knowledge and experience, with a deep desire to support children and families to thrive.

www.ingramcontent.com/pod-product-compliance
Lightning Source LLC
Chambersburg PA
CBRC091202070526
44583CB00008B/181